What Can I...

Taste

Sue Barraclough

Chicago, Illinois

© 2005 Raintree
Published by Raintree, an imprint of Capstone Global Library, LLC
Chicago, Illinois
Customer Service 888-363-4266
Visit our website at www.raintreelibrary.com

Printed and bound by South China Printing Company.
12 11
10 9 8 7 6 5

Library of Congress Cataloging-in-Publication Data:
Barraclough, Sue.
  What can I taste? / Sue Barraclough.
    p. cm. -- (What can I?)
  Includes index.
  ISBN 1-4109-2166-2 (library binding-hardcover) -- ISBN 1-4109-2172-7
(pbk.) ISBN 978-1-4109-2166-6 (library binding-hardcover) -- ISBN 978-1-4109-2172-7 (pbk.)
 1. Taste--Juvenile literature. I. Title: Taste?. II. Title. III.
Series: Barraclough, Sue. What can I?
  QP456.B37 2005
  612.8'7--dc22

                        2004026303

Acknowledgments
The publishers would like to thank the following for permission to reproduce photographs: Corbis p.**19** left and right insets; Eyewire p.**11**; Getty Images/PhotoDisc p.**23** top inset; Harcourt Education pp.**6-7**, **12** top inset, **14**(Gareth Boden), **10**, **12** bottom inset, **15** (Trevor Clifford), **4-5**, **8-9**, **16**, **17**, **18**, **19**, **20-21**, **22**(Tudor Photography); Punchstock pp.**12-13**.

Cover photograph reproduced with permission of Harcourt Education Ltd. / Tudor Photography.

Every effort has been made to contact copyright holders of any material reproduced in this book. Any omissions will be rectified in subsequent printings if notice is given to the publishers.

Some words are shown in bold, **like this**. You can find out what they mean by looking in the glossary on page 24.

Contents

Breakfast Tastes

Toast tastes delicious with strawberry jam.

What is your favorite breakfast taste?

ROBERTSON'S

ROSE'S
Orange Fine Cut
Marmalade

454g

Toothpaste Tastes

Toothpaste tastes fresh and clean.

Cheesy Tastes

Do you like the taste of cheese?

Some cheeses have a very **powerful** taste and smell.

Fruity Tastes

Look at all the fruit. Some fruit tastes sweet. Some tastes sour.

How do lemons taste?

Ice cream is sweet and cold.

Chocolate

Strawberry

Vanilla

What flavor is your favorite?

Picnic Tastes

Which picnic food would you eat first?

Is there anything here you would not want to taste?

Party Food

Preparing party food is fun...

...but tasting
everything is the
best part!

Birthday Tastes

What flavor do you think this cake is?

Tasty Games

Can you guess what each thing tastes like?

Chips are salty.

Lemon is sour.

Chocolate is sweet.

18

Apples taste **juicy** and sweet.

splash!

Party treats

Everyone takes treats home from a birthday party.

Which party bag would you choose?

sweet

salty

sour

...or salty things,
and sour things.
Good night!

Glossary

juicy   full of juice
powerful   very strong
preparing   getting ready

Index

Notes for Adults

Books in the *What Can I...* series encourage children to use their senses to actively explore the world around them.

Additional Information
The tongue is covered in small bumps called taste buds. The taste buds are made up of cells that detect flavour. There are four main tastes – sweet, sour, salty, and bitter, and each one is detected on a different area of the tongue.

Follow-up Activities
• Ask children what foods they enjoy and which ones they dislike. Ask children to explain why they dislike some foods but like others.

• Set up a tasting station in the room with simple foods like apples, chocolate, carrots, etc. Make sure none of the children is allergic to the foods you set out. Then ask each child to close his or her eyes and taste the foods. Ask them if they can tell what each food is by its taste.